Start-Up
Connections
EATING FRUIT AND VEGETABLES

Claire Llewellyn

Evans

Evans Brothers Limited

First published in this edition in 2010

Published by Evans Brothers Limited
2A Portman Mansions
Chiltern Street
London W1U 6NR

Produced for Evans Brothers Limited by
White-Thomson Publishing Ltd.,
+44 (0) 843 2087 460
www.wtpub.co.uk

Printed & bound in China by New Era Printing
Company Limited

Editor: Dereen Taylor
Consultants: Nina Siddall, Head of Primary School
Improvement, East Sussex; Norah Granger, former
primary head teacher and senior lecturer in Education,
University of Brighton; Kate Ruttle, freelance literacy
consultant and Literacy Co-ordinator, Special Needs
Co-ordinator, and Deputy Headteacher at a primary
school in Suffolk.
Designer: Leishman Design
Cover design: Balley Design Limited

British Library Cataloguing in Publication Data

Llewellyn, Claire.
    Eating fruit and vegetables. -- (Start-up connections)
    1. Nutrition--Juvenile literature. 2. Fruit--Juvenile
    literature. 3. Vegetables--Juvenile literature.
    I. Title II. Series
    613.2-dc22

ISBN: 978 0 237 54174 3

Acknowledgements:
Special thanks to the following for their help and
involvement in the preparation of this book: Staff and
pupils at Coldean Primary School, Brighton and Elm
Grove Primary School, Brighton.

Picture Acknowledgements:
Chris Fairclough 4 (bottom), 7 (bottom), 9 (bottom), 10,
11 (top), 12, 13, 14, 15 (top), 17, 20. Liz Price cover, title
page, 4 (top), 5, 6, 7 (top), 8, 9 (top), 11 (bottom), 15
(bottom), 18, 21.

Artwork:
Tom Price age 8, page 16; Hattie Spilsbury age 10,
page 19.

Contents

Examining fruit and vegetables

Dan and Emily are looking at fruit and vegetables. They examine the outside to find out if the skin is rough or smooth. Which ones smell?

◀ Which fruit and vegetables are juicy inside? Which ones have seeds? Which ones have a strong smell?

rough   smooth   smell

The children put their answers on a chart.

	kiwi fruit	avocado	melon	tomato
strong smell		✔	✔	
juicy inside	✔		✔	✔
seeds	✔	✔	✔	✔

Fruit and vegetables come in different colours. Look in the supermarket to see which colour is the most common. How could you show this on a chart?

juicy   seeds   colours   5

Describing fruit and vegetables

There are many different words to describe fruit and vegetables.

"This tomato is small, red and round. It feels firm."

▲ Some words describe the way they look and feel.

"This mandarin smells tangy and has a sweet, fresh taste."

▲ Some words describe the way they smell and taste.

6   describe   feels   firm   look

"Cucumber feels wet. When you bite it, it's crunchy."

Some words describe the way they feel in your mouth.

crisp crunchy firm
small long stringy
juicy bumpy hard
sweet squashy
round sour

▶ **Which words would you choose to describe the fruit and vegetables in the picture?**

fresh   taste   bite   crunchy   **7**

Making fruit kebabs

Tom is making fruit kebabs out of kiwi fruits, apples and strawberries. Fruit kebabs are a healthy snack.

▶ Tom washes the fruit and drains it in a colander.

◀ Tom peels the kiwi fruit. He also chops the apples and slices the stalks off the strawberries.

HYGIENE!
Always wash your hands before touching food.

WARNING!
Knives and skewers are sharp. Use them with care.

healthy   snack   washes   drains

▶ **Tom mixes the fruit on wooden skewers. Which fruit kebab looks best? Why?**

◀ **Do you recognise the kitchen tools in the picture? What would you use them for?**

Can you think up a new kitchen tool? What job would it do? How could you make it?

peels   chops   tools

Investigating packaging

Some fruit and vegetables are
fresh. Others have been frozen,
dried, tinned, or made
into juice.

These foods are packaged to
protect them from germs and bumps.
What kinds of packaging can you see in the picture?

frozen   dried   tinned

Kayla's class plan to sell fruit on sports day. The fruit must look attractive and be clean and fresh. How could they package it?

▶ Which of these items of packaging could they use?

juice   packaging   attractive   11

Taste tests

We prepare fruit and vegetables in different ways. Some foods can be eaten raw. Ali is tasting some mashed, baked and fresh banana.

"This looks and tastes like baby food. I don't like it."

"This is warm and soft. It's ok, but the taste is a bit strong."

prepare   raw   mashed

"I enjoy eating bananas like this. They're yummy."

Why not try the following carrot taste test?

1 Raw carrot, washed and peeled.

2 Grated carrot, mixed with lemon juice and salt and pepper.

3 Boiled carrot.

Which do you think you would like best?

baked   grated   boiled   13

Making healthy soups and drinks

▶ Vegetables can be used to make soups. You can add pasta, too.

Some vegetable soups have bits in them. Other soups are put in a blender and whizzed until they are smooth. Which kind of soups do you prefer?

soups   blender   prefer

Fruit can be put in a blender, too. It can be mixed with milk or yogurt to make drinks called smoothies.

▼ Tom and Emily are having smoothies.

Which fruits would you like in your smoothie?

smoothies

A healthy diet

Fruit and vegetables are good for us. They help to keep us fit. They are part of a healthy diet.

Monday	Tuesday	Wednesday	Thursday	Friday

◀ Fatima kept a fruit and vegetable diary. When did she eat the most fruit and vegetables? When did she eat the least?

Factbox

We should try to eat five pieces of fruit and vegetables a day.

fit   diet   most   least

▶ Fatima asked her friends how many fruit and vegetables they eat every day.

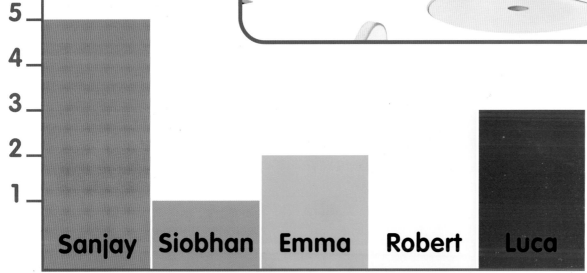

She made a **bar chart** of the results.
Who has five pieces a day? Who has just one?

pieces   bar chart

Planning a picnic

Ria's class are planning
a Teddy Bears' Picnic.

"We need food like sandwiches that we can carry easily."

"I'd like some fruit juice in case I get thirsty."

HYGIENE!

Wash your hands before touching food.

Lettuce
Cheese
Butter
Bread

Colander
Chopping Board
Vegetable knife
Butter knife
Bread knife
Grater
plastic Box.

► They want to make sandwiches. They make lists of the things they will need.

picnic   thirsty

How to make cheese and lettuce sandwiches

▲ Wash and drain the lettuce.

▲ Butter the bread.

▲ Grate the cheese.

▲ Add some lettuce.

▲ Add another piece of bread and cut in half.

▲ Put the sandwiches in a plastic box.

WARNING! Knives are sharp. Use them with care.

carry   plastic

Choosing fruit for the picnic

Charmaine and Ali are thinking about fruit for the picnic. They want it to look and taste nice, and be easy to eat. They don't want fruit that will get squashed.

▲ Which of these fruits do you think would be best for the picnic?

easy   squashed

The children enjoy their Teddy Bears' Picnic.
What do they say about the food and drink?

water   better   hungry

Further information for Parents and Teachers

FRUIT AND VEGETABLES ACTIVITY PAGE

Use the activities on these pages to help you to make the most of *Eating Fruit and Vegetables.*

Activities suggested on this page support progression in learning by consolidating and developing ideas from the book and helping the children to link the new concepts with their own experiences. Making these links is crucial in helping young children to engage with learning and to become lifelong learners.

Ideas on the next page develop essential skills for learning by suggesting ways of making links across the curriculum and in particular to literacy, personal development and ICT.

WORD PANEL

Check that the children know the meaning of each of these words from the book.

attractive	describe	frozen	pips/seeds
bitter	diet	healthy	prefer
blender	drain	juice	prepare
boil	dried	mash	raw
chop	firm	packaging	squashed
crunchy	fresh	peel	tinned

DESCRIBING FRUIT AND VEGETABLES

Help children to develop a vocabulary for describing fruit and vegetables.

- Provide whole fruit and vegetables. Ask children to write descriptive words on sticky notes. Encourage them to use 3 senses: touch, smell, sight. Take photos of the fruits and vegetables.
- Supervise some children while they cut the fruit and vegetables. Encourage then to use all five senses when describing what they're experiencing. Take photos of the insides of the fruit and vegetables.
- Ask other children to match the photographs of the insides and the outsides of the fruit and vegetables.
- Make a display of the photographs, together with the best of the children's describing words.

PREPARING AND EATING FOOD

Give children opportunities to follow some of the recipes and ideas in the book.

- Talk first about issues around hygiene and safety. Ensure that children understand why the rules are important.
- Ask them to rewrite the recount text on pages 8 and 9 as a recipe, then make their own fruit kebabs.
- Show them how to find simple and appropriate recipes on the internet.
- Talk about the importance of the presentation of food. Look through recipe books together and discuss whether they would rather eat well presented food, or food that was all mixed up on the plate.

SUPERMARKETS

If possible, visit a supermarket and look at their fruit and vegetables section.

- Talk about how the fruit and vegetables are displayed. Is it attractive or not? How could it be improved?
- Discuss the layout inside the shop - why are carrots near potatoes and apples nearer to oranges?
- Look at the packaging. Talk about which foods are packaged and why. Evaluate the packaging: which looks attractive? Which is protecting the produce?
- Is there a weighing scales nearby? Demonstrate how to use them and talk about why people use them.
- Look for fruit and vegetables in other parts of the shop, for example in freezer and chiller cabinets, the baking section, in tins, sauces, drinks.

SHOPPING FOR FRUIT AND VEGETABLES

Set up a role play greengrocer's shop.

- Ask children to weigh with the hands to determine comparative weights of a variety of fruits and vegetables. Show them how to use balance scales to verify their judgements.
- Make an interactive 'weight line'. Use mini-pegs to attach labels and weights of fruit and vegetables. Keep real examples of the fruit and vegetables under the weight line so that children get used to feeling a weight while they're looking at the number.

USING EATING FRUIT AND VEGETABLES FOR CROSS CURRICULAR WORK

The revised national curriculum focuses on children developing key competencies as

- successful learners
- confident individuals and
- responsible citizens.

Cross curricular work is particularly beneficial in developing the thinking and learning skills that contribute to building these competencies because it encourages children to make links, to transfer learning skills and to apply knowledge from one context to another. As importantly, cross curricular work can help children to understand how school work links to their daily lives. For many children, this is a key motivation in becoming a learner.

The web below indicates some areas for cross curricular study. Others may well come from your own class's engagement with the ideas in the book.

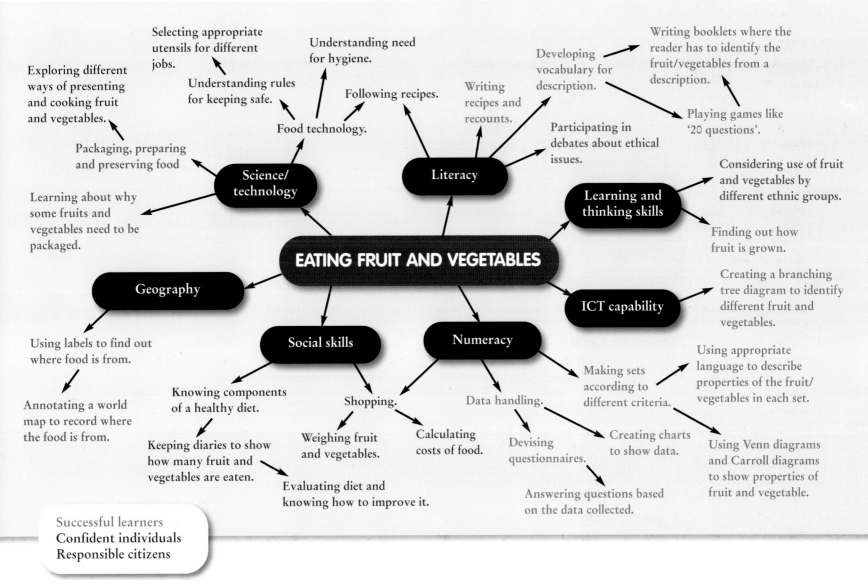

Successful learners
Confident individuals
Responsible citizens

Index